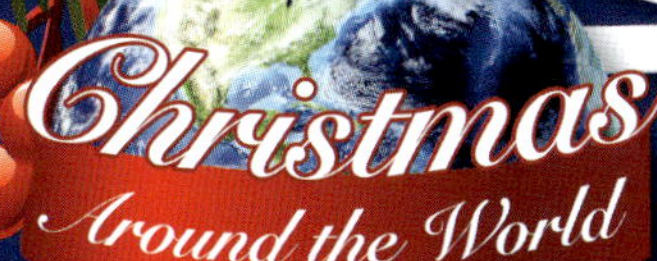

Mexico

By Christina Earley

Table of Contents

A Starfish Book

Teaching Tips for Caregivers:

As a caregiver, you can help your child succeed in school by giving them a strong foundation in language and literacy skills and a desire to learn to read.

This book helps children grow by letting them practice reading skills.

Reading for pleasure and interest will help your child to develop reading skills and will give your child the opportunity to practice these skills in meaningful ways.

- Encourage your child to read on her own at home
- Encourage your child to practice reading aloud
- Encourage activities that require reading
- Establish a reading time
- Talk with your child
- Give your child writing materials

Teaching Tips for Teachers:

Research shows that one of the best ways for students to learn a new topic is to read about it.

Before Reading

- Read the "Words to Know" and discuss the meaning of each word.
- Read the back cover to see what the book is about.

During Reading

- When a student gets to a word that is unknown, ask them to look at the rest of the sentence to find clues to help with the meaning of the unknown word.
- Ask the student to write down any pages of the book that were confusing to them.

After Reading

- Discuss the main idea of the book.
- Ask students to give one detail that they learned in the book by showing a text dependent answer from the book.

Christmas in Mexico

FELIZ NAVIDAD

Christmas is celebrated in Mexico.

The season is from December 12th to January 6th.

Families put out **nativities**.

They show the Christmas story.

Fun Fact:
The nativity scenes are called *nacimientos*.

Children go from home to home during Las Posadas. They carry statues of Mary, Joseph, and a donkey.

Fun Fact:
Las Posadas means "The Inns" in Spanish.

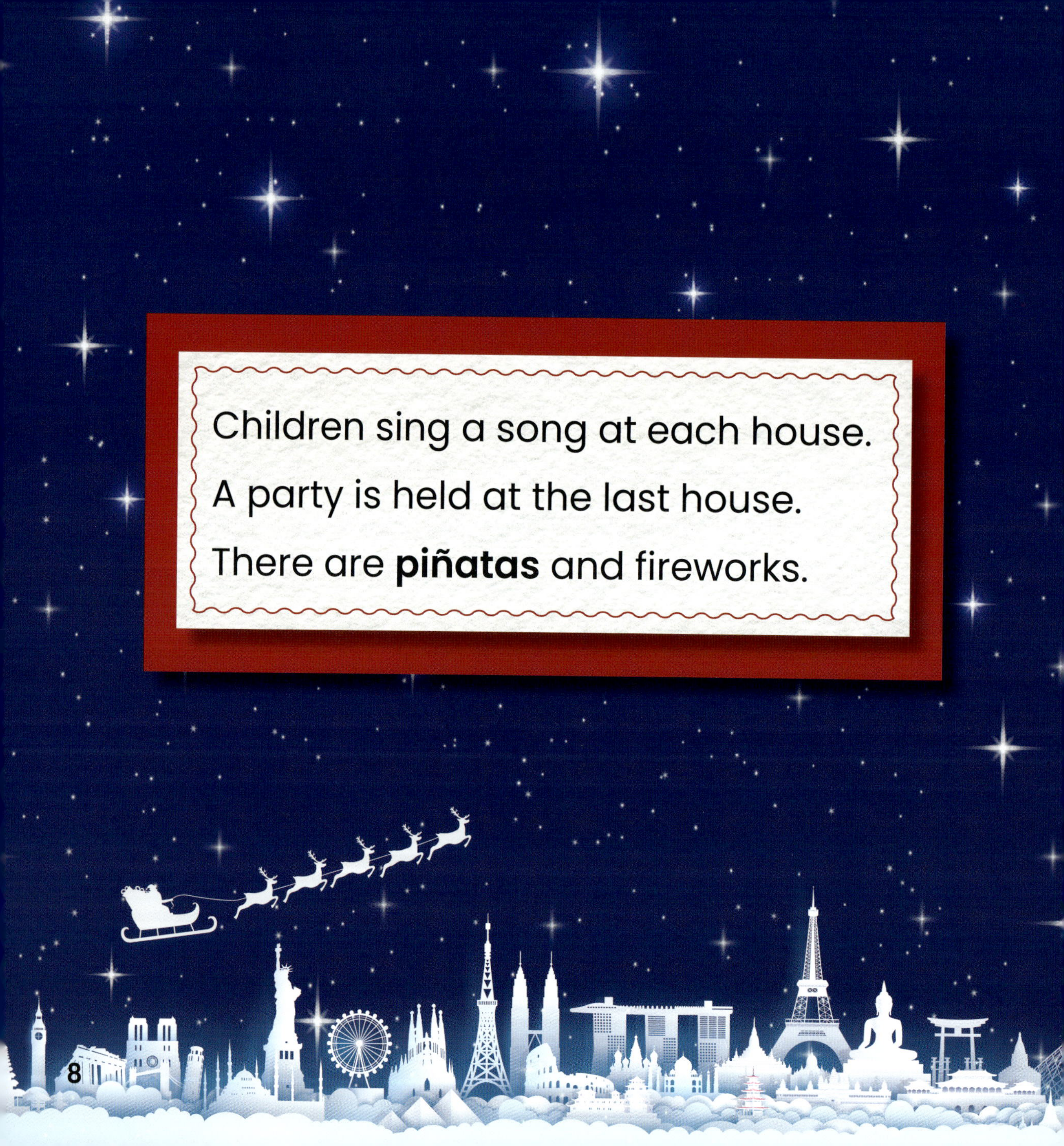

Children sing a song at each house.
A party is held at the last house.
There are **piñatas** and fireworks.

Special foods are eaten on Christmas Eve.

Pozole is a tasty soup.

Buñuelos are a sweet treat.

Pozole
Buñuelos

Families go to church at midnight on Christmas Eve.

Fireworks light the sky to start Christmas Day.

Baby Jesus and Santa Claus bring gifts on Christmas Eve.

Many children get gifts from the Three **Kings**.

Fun Fact:
Día de los Reyes, or Three Kings Day, is on January 6th.

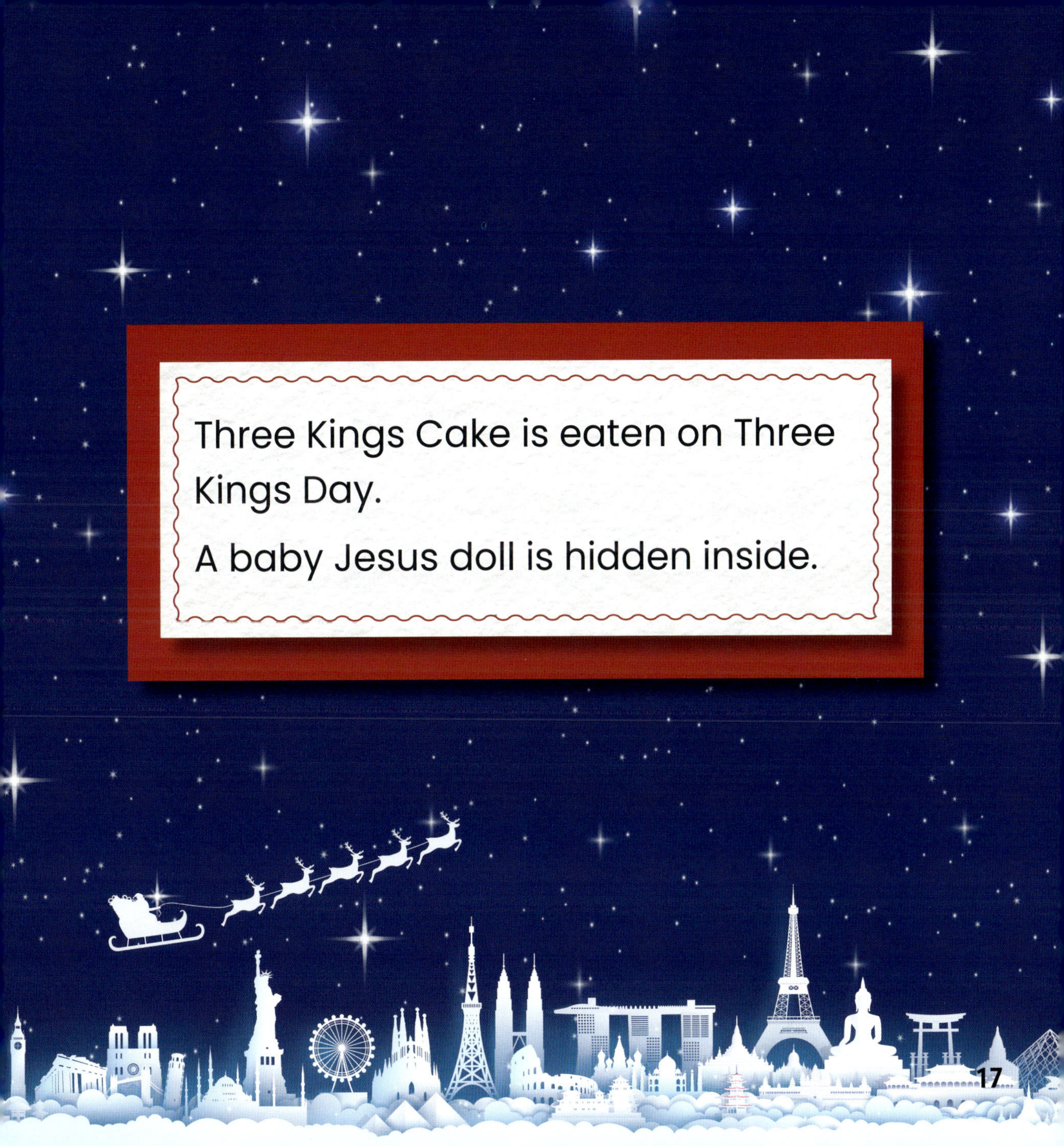

Three Kings Cake is eaten on Three Kings Day.

A baby Jesus doll is hidden inside.

The **poinsettia** is the Christmas Eve flower. The shape of the leaves looks like a star.

Fun Fact:
A legend explains how a little girl's gift of weeds became the poinsettia.

Craft: Christmas Poinsettia

Materials

- 5 white, round coffee filters
- washable markers: green, yellow, red, and pink
- cookie sheet, wax paper, or freezer paper
- old towels
- spray bottle with water
- pencil
- scissors
- glue
- sparkly gold pom-poms

Steps

1. Flatten the coffee filters.
2. Color one coffee filter with green and yellow washable markers.
3. Color four coffee filters with red and pink washable markers.
4. Place the coffee filters on the cookie sheet or wax/freezer paper with old towels underneath.
5. Lightly spray the coffee filters with water. Let dry.
6. Draw large flower shapes on two red/pink coffee filters. (See the picture.) Cut them out.
7. Draw small flower shapes on two red/pink coffee filters. (See the picture.) Cut them out.
8. With a red marker, outline the petals and add details.
9. Cut leaf shapes from the green/yellow filter.
10. Use a green marker to outline the leaves and add details.
11. Place the two large flowers on top of each other with top and bottom petals alternating. Glue in the center.
12. Place and glue the smaller flowers on top of the larger ones. Scrunch the flower slightly to add dimension. Let dry.
13. Glue the leaves to the back.
14. Glue the sparkly pom-poms in the center.

Recipe: Ensalada Nochebuena (Christmas Eve Salad)

Ingredients

Salad:

- ½ head romaine lettuce, chopped
- 2 medium cooked beets, sliced
- 1 ripe plantain or banana, sliced
- 1 cup jicama or water chestnuts, diced
- 1 large, sweet apple, cut into wedges
- 1 large orange, peeled and cut into sections
- ½ cup unsalted peanuts
- 1 cup pomegranate seeds

Dressing:

- ¼ cup orange juice
- 2 tablespoons red wine vinegar
- 1 tablespoon olive oil
- 1 tablespoon fresh mint or 1 teaspoon dried mint
- ⅛ teaspoon salt
- honey or sugar to taste

Steps

1. Place chopped lettuce on a large serving platter or in a clear salad bowl.
2. Put the sliced beets over the lettuce in a single layer.
3. Layer the other fruits and vegetables over the lettuce.
4. Sprinkle the top with peanuts and pomegranate seeds.
5. In a separate small bowl, combine dressing ingredients.
6. Just before serving, drizzle the dressing over the salad.

Words to Know

buñuelos (boo-noo-EH-lowz): fried dough fritters covered with sugar and cinnamon

inns (ins): places where people can stay when away from their homes; in the Christmas story, Joseph and Mary could not find a room at an inn

kings (kingz): male rulers of royal birth; in the Christmas story, three kings traveled to visit baby Jesus

nativities (nuh-TIV-i-tees): stable scenes that show baby Jesus, Mary, Joseph, animals, shepherds, and angels

piñatas (puhn-YAH-tuhs): decorated figures filled with candy or toys that are hit by a stick to break open

poinsettia (poin-SET-ee-uh): a small shrub with dark red leaves around small yellow flowers

Index

Comprehension Questions

1. During Las Posadas, children
   a. sing.
   b. read.
   c. play soccer.

2. The Christmas season lasts from
   a. December 24th to January 2nd.
   b. December 24th to December 25th.
   c. December 12th to January 6th.

3. A special soup served on Christmas Eve is
   a. Las Posadas.
   b. nacimientos.
   c. pozole.

4. True or false: Only Santa Claus brings gifts to children.

5. True or false: The poinsettia is known as the Christmas Eve flower.

Answers
1. a 2. c 3. c 4. False 5. True

About the Author

Christina Earley lives in South Florida with her with husband, son, and dog named Bailey. Her favorite holiday is Christmas because it is a magical time of year. She collects ornaments that remind her of special places and events. She and her family have lots of fun baking cookies and eating candy canes while looking at Christmas lights.

Written by: Christina Earley
Design by: Jen Bowers
Editor: Kim Thompson

Library of Congress PCN Data
Christmas in Mexico / Earley
Christmas Around the World
ISBN 978-1-63897-441-3 (hard cover)
ISBN 978-1-63897-556-4 (paperback)
ISBN 978-1-63897-671-4 (EPUB)
ISBN 978-1-63897-786-5 (eBook)
Library of Congress Control Number: 2022930311

Photographs: Cover ©2015 Bill Perry/Shutterstock, pine ©Pasko Maksim/Shutterstock,world skyline©Painterstock/Shutterstock, background©ghenadie/Shutterstock, earth ©leonello/iStock; p.1 ©Mariana Mast/Shutterstock; p.3 ©2012 ESB Professional/Shutterstock; p.5© 2017 Ulrike Stein/Shutterstock, ornament©ekler/Shutterstock; p.7 ©2013 ChiccoDodiFC/Shutterstock; p.9 ©2018 clicksdemexico/Shutterstock; p.11 ©2019 Guajillo studio/Shutterstock, ©2020 Guajillo studio/Shutterstock; p.13 ©2018 stacyarturogi/Shutterstock; p.14 ©2012 Anneka/Shutterstock; p.15 ©2016 phatymak's studio/Shutterstock; p.16 ©2021 Marcos Castillo/Shutterstock, ©2021 Rosamar/Shutterstock; p.19 ©2021 PandaStudio/Shutterstock; p.20 ©makiaki/Shutterstock; p.21 ©2021 Cbeamglitter/Shutterstock

Printed in the United States of America.

Seahorse Publishing Company
www.seahorsepub.com

Published in the United States
Seahorse Publishing
PO Box 771325
Coral Springs, FL 33077